ADORABLE
APPLE DUMPLIN'S BOOK

An "Everything Apple" Adventure

by Nicole Okaty

Scholastic Inc.

New York   Toronto   London   Auckland   Sydney   Mexico City   New Delhi   Hong Kong   Buenos Aires

ISBN 0-439-70310-7

Designer: Emily Muschinske
Illustrations: Lisa and Terry Workman
Photographs: Nicole Okaty

12 11 10 9 8 7 6 5 4 3 2 1   4 5 6 7 8 9/0

Printed in the U.S.A.
First Scholastic printing, October 2004

TABLE of CONTENTS

Get Ready for an
ALL-APPLE ADVENTURE!

Hi, my berry sweet friend! It's me, Strawberry Shortcake and my adorable little sister, Apple Dumplin'.

Uh huh.

We're going on an applicious crafts, games, and recipes adventure, and we're so berry glad that you are coming with us!

Yippee!

Apple Ducklin'— Apple Dumplin's berry best pet pal— will be joining us, too.

My Ducklin'!

So grab your Apple Craft Kit and let's get started!

Strawberry Shortcake's Tips for Getting Started

1. Set up a space of your berry own where you can spread out and create your apple-activities!

2. Collect the materials you'll need before starting a new project.

3. Whenever you see this symbol throughout the book, it means that you can find what you need in your craft kit.

4. Some of the materials you'll need can be found around your house. You can get the other materials at your grocery or craft store.

5. Put on an apron or an art smock before beginning a project that could get messy—like painting or making applesauce cinnamon dough.

6. You may need an adult's help with some activities in the book. Whenever you see this symbol, you'll know to ask for help.

Getting Ready to Create With Apples

Many of the crafts and recipes in this book use fresh apples. Here are a few tips:

1. When picking apples, look for ones that are bright, shiny, and firm.

2. Store apples in the refrigerator, and use them within a few weeks.

3. Wash the apples in cold water before you eat them.

4. Always ask an adult to core and cut the apples for you.

5. Save 8 or so apple seeds from your apples. You'll use them to play a berry fun game you'll find on pages 22 and 23 of this book!

Getting Ready to Paint

1. Place newspaper on the area where you'll be painting.

2. Have a small bowl of water and some paper towels handy for easy clean up, especially if you plan to change paint colors during a project.

3. When you mix two different colors of paint together, you can make a whole new color. In this book, you'll mix red and yellow paint to make Apple Ducklin's orange webbed feet!

red   yellow   orange

4. You'll use a special art sponge in some of the projects. For best results, moisten the sponge and squeeze out the extra water before you dip it into the paint. Then, stamp the sponge onto your paper and lift the sponge straight up.

Red Delicious Apples

This delicious apple painting is made by printing a real apple!

1. Start with a well-shaped Red Delicious apple. Wash it in cold water, and dry it with a paper towel.

2. With an adult's help, cut the apple in half the long way. You'll only need half of the apple for your painting. So go ahead and eat the other half as a snack!

What You Need

- Red Delicious apple
- Paper towel
- Cutting knife
- Red washable paint
- Paper plate
- Paintbrush
- 1 sheet of light-green or other light-colored construction paper
- Markers or crayons (green and brown)

3. Pour red paint the size of a strawberry onto a paper plate, and stir it with your paintbrush.

4. Dip the flat part of your apple into the red paint. Brush the paint on evenly with your paintbrush.

5. Press the paint-covered side of your apple down hard onto a light-green sheet of paper. Lift the apple straight up. Make as many prints as you like, painting on more paint, if needed.

6. Add green leaves and brown stems to your apples, using markers or crayons.

Here's More: The Red Delicious apple is one of America's favorite snacking apples. Granny Smith and McIntosh apples are also popular.

Which kind of apples do you like best? Collect a variety and have a taste test with your berry best friends to decide!

Turn the page to make a painting of Apple Dumplin's cute duck!

Printing Apple Ducklin'

This berry sweet duck is the apple of Apple Dumplin's eye!

What You Need

- Red Delicious apple
- Paper towel
- Cutting knife
- Washable paint (in yellow, red, green, and orange)
- Paper plate
- Paintbrush
- 1 sheet of construction paper (any light color is fine)

1. Wash a well-shaped Red Delicious apple in cold water, and dry it. With an adult's help, cut the apple into quarters the long way, and remove the seeds. You'll only need one quarter of the apple for your painting. So go ahead and eat the rest as a snack!

2. Arrange the paint colors—yellow, orange, green, and red—on a paper plate. You'll need yellow paint and orange paint about the size of a strawberry, and a blueberry-sized amount of red and green paint. See page 5 to remember how to make orange paint.

8

3. Dip one flat side of your apple wedge into the yellow paint. Brush the paint on evenly with your paintbrush.

6. Add Apple Ducklin's red bow, green eyes, orange-webbed feet, and triangular bill.

4. Lay your paper down the tall way. Press the apple onto the paper to make the duck's body. Lift the apple straight up.

Here's More: You can paint Apple Ducklin' standing on some grass.

5. Dip your paintbrush into the yellow paint again. Round out the body, and add a bell-shaped head and tail feathers. Let dry.

You'll use a berry special art sponge to make the next painting!

A is for Apple

This juicy red apple is made by sponging an apple-shaped stencil!

What You Need

- Pencil
- 5-x-5-inch piece of construction paper
- Scissors
- 1 sheet of bright-yellow construction paper
- Washable paint (in red and green)
- Paper plate
- Art sponge
- Paintbrush
- Optional: Tape

1. **What size and shape will your apple be? With your pencil, draw an apple shape onto a piece of construction paper.**

2. **With an adult's help, push a hole through the center of your apple drawing with the pencil, and cut the inside of the shape out to make your stencil.**

3. Take your yellow construction paper and turn it sideways. Tape the stencil down to the center of the paper, if you like.

4. Pour a strawberry-sized amount of red paint and a blueberry-sized amount of green paint onto a paper plate.

5. Paint the apple's skin red by dipping the art sponge into the red paint. Fill in the inside of your stencil by smearing the sponge several times. Repeat for the green leaves, washing the sponge first. Let the paint dry.

6. Carefully remove the tape and your stencil. Use a paintbrush to touch up the apple shape, if needed.

Here's More: See if you can think of some apple sayings and find out what they mean! How about,

"An apple a day keeps the doctor away!"
or
"You're the apple of my eye!"

Turn the page for more color-filled fun!

11

Applicious Lunch Bag

These colorful apples look adorable on a brown lunch bag!

1. Draw an apple shape onto each of the three pieces of card stock or construction paper, using your pencil.

What You Need

- Pencil
- Three 3-x-3-inch pieces of card stock or construction paper
- Scissors
- Washable paint (in red, green, and yellow)
- Paper plate
- Tape
- Brown or white paper lunch bag
- Art sponge
- Markers or crayons (green and brown)
- Hole punch
- 20 inches of ribbon or yarn

2. With an adult's help, push a hole through the center of your three apple drawings with a pencil, and cut the inside of the shapes out to make three stencils.

3. Pour a strawberry-sized amount of red, green, and yellow paint onto a paper plate. You will use one stencil per color.

4. Tape your apple stencils onto the paper bag any way you like.

7. Using markers or crayons, add green leaves and brown stems to the apples.

5. Dip the art sponge into one color of paint and fill in the inside of your stencil. Make sure to wash the sponge before using another color!

8. Fold the top of the lunch bag over and punch two holes, as shown. Lace the ribbon or yarn through the holes, and tie the bag closed by making a pretty bow.

6. Let the paint dry. Carefully remove the tape and your stencils. Your picture will stay! Add as many apples as you like.

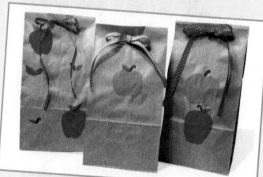

Turn the page to see who likes to play Follow the Leader with Apple Dumplin'!

13

Apple Ducklin' Paper Doll Chain

These little ducks need Apple Dumplin' to lead the way!

What You Need

- 6-x-24-inch sheet of white rectangular paper or a cut-open brown paper bag
- Pencil
- Scissors
- Markers or crayons (any colors)
- Tape

1. To make an Apple Ducklin' paper doll chain, fold the large sheet of white paper or brown paper bag like a fan—back and forth. The folds need to be as wide as you want your ducks to be (about 4 1/2 inches).

2. Using a pencil, draw a duck shape onto one side of the paper fan, so that the duck's bill and tail feathers go a little bit off the paper.

3. With an adult's help, cut out the duck shape, cutting through all the layers at once. Don't cut through the folds at the tail and beak, or you won't make a chain.

Berry Funny

Q: What apple isn't an apple?

A: A pineapple!

4. Unfold your paper and decorate the ducks any way you want with markers or crayons.

Here's More: Now that you know how, you can create other paper doll figures, too. Will you make a chain of people holding hands? It's up to you!

5. Use tape to hang your Apple Ducklin' paper doll chain up in your room!

Turn the page to see one of Apple Dumplin's favorite rides!

Apple Dumplin's Fun-filled Wagon

Apple Dumplin' and I have taken this fun-filled wagon on many applicious adventures!

What You Need

- 1 sheet of light-colored construction paper
- 4 craft sticks
- White craft glue or school glue
- Fine-point markers (in red, yellow, and green)
- Pencil
- Optional: Round candy in bright apple colors (red, green, and yellow)

1. Lay your sheet of construction paper sideways. Glue one craft stick to the center of your paper the long way, as shown.

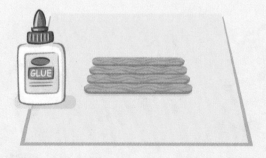

2. Then, add the other three sticks, one by one, below the first craft stick, until all are glued down.

3. Color the four craft sticks, using the markers.

4. Draw two quarter-sized circles (wagon wheels) underneath the bottom craft stick. The circles should be about 2 inches apart.

5. Color the wagon wheels any way you like. You can add apples on the wheels, too.

6. Draw and color a handle on your wagon.

Here's More: You can fill your wagon with "apples" by gluing on round candy in bright apple colors! Or, you can use buttons, or draw and color some "apples" of your own!

Turn the page to see how the next project pops off the paper!

Apple Dumplin's Pop-Up Apple Tree

This tissue paper apple tree is as colorful as the ones in Strawberryland!

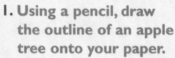

1. Using a pencil, draw the outline of an apple tree onto your paper.

What You Need

- Pencil with an eraser
- 1 sheet of sky-blue construction paper
- Scissors
- Tissue paper (in light green, dark green, brown, and red)
- White craft glue or school glue
- Paper plate

2. With an adult's help, cut the light green, dark green, and red tissue paper into about 2-x-2-inch squares. You'll need to cut out more green squares (leaves) than red squares (apples).

3. Cut a piece of brown tissue paper in half. Fold one side and roll it into a tree trunk. Trim the trunk to fit your page.

4. Glue the trunk on top of your apple tree outline. Use more brown tissue paper to fill in the branches of your tree.

5. Pour a small amount of glue onto a paper plate. To make the tree's leaves, take the pencil's eraser, twist the green tissue paper squares around the end of it, and dip them into the glue.

6. Glue the green paper pieces onto the treetop, one by one, so that the paper stands up. Will your tree's leaves be mostly light green or dark green? You decide.

7. To make the apples, twist the red paper squares around the end of the eraser, and dip them into the glue.

8. Glue the red paper pieces onto the treetop, one by one. Press the paper down, and shape the pieces into round apples with your eraser.

9. Fill in the treetop with apples and leaves, until it's the shape you want it to be.

There's a berry starry sky waiting for you on the next page!

19

Twinkle, Twinkle, Apple Star

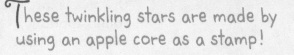

These twinkling stars are made by using an apple core as a stamp!

What You Need

- Red Delicious apples
- Apple corer
- Yellow washable paint
- Paper plate
- Paintbrush
- 1 sheet of blue paper

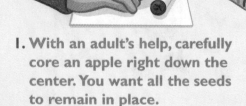

1. With an adult's help, carefully core an apple right down the center. You want all the seeds to remain in place.

2. To make your apple stampers, ask an adult to cut the apple core in half through the middle. Gently remove the seeds. If you look at both halves of the apple core, you'll discover that each one has a five-pointed star.

3. Pour yellow paint, about the size of a strawberry, onto a paper plate. Dip half the apple core into the paint. Blot the paint lightly with a paintbrush, so that you can see the star shape.

4. Press (stamp) the apple core firmly onto your blue paper. Lift the core straight up. Repeat, using more paint, to make as many sparkling stars as you like.

Apple Dumplin's
Apple-Seed-Toss Board Game

This game is played by tossing apple seeds onto a game board.
You and a friend earn points when seeds land on squares of your color.
The player with the most points after her toss wins!

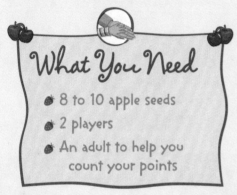

What You Need

- 8 to 10 apple seeds
- 2 players
- An adult to help you count your points

1. Each player selects a color from the game board on pages 22 and 23—pink for Strawberry Shortcake and green for Apple Dumplin'.

2. Player 1 tosses a handful of 8 to 10 apple seeds onto the board and counts the number of seeds that fall on her color. For every seed that falls on that color, Player 1 earns one point. For every seed that falls on the other player's color, Player 1 earns zero points.

3. There are two berry special squares on the game board—one is a Strawberry Shortcake square, and the other is an Apple Dumplin' square. If an apple seed lands on your character, you get double points for that toss! For instance, if one of your seeds lands on your character, you earn 2 points. If 2 seeds land on your character, you earn 4 points!

4. Then, it's Player 2's turn, who plays the same way as Player 1.

5. Whoever has the most points from their apple seed toss wins! Now play again—winner goes first!

Here's More: You can play this game in two ways:
1) The player with the most points after each player tosses once wins!
2) You can play this game in several rounds and tally up your points. For instance, whoever earns the most points in 3 rounds wins!

Will you toss your apple seeds from high above or close to the game board? Will you toss your apple seeds slowly or quickly? You decide! Take a few practice tosses before you play, to see what works best for you!

Apple Dumplin's Apple Cake Adventure

Angel Cake and I are getting together to make one of Apple Dumplin's favorite desserts—an apple cake.

Can you find everything on these two pages that begins with the letter "A"—like apple—before the cake is ready? Hint: There are 14 "A" things to find.

(Turn to page 38 for the answers.)

24

My Favorite Animals

Turn the page for some berry bubbly outdoor fun!

25

Apple Dumplin's Berry Fun Apple Bubbles

These bubbles smell just like apples.
Catch a bubble if you can!

What You Need

- Sealable plastic container
- 2 cups of warm water
- ¼ cup light corn syrup
- 1 teaspoon sugar
- Spoon
- ½ cup apple-scented or other dishwashing liquid
- Pipe cleaner

1. In a sealable plastic container, add the warm water, light corn syrup, and sugar.

2. Using a spoon, stir in the dishwashing liquid, until the ingredients are blended.

3. What size would you like your
   bubbles to be? Form one end of your
   pipe cleaner into a circle. If you want
   to make small bubbles, make the
   circle small. If you want to make
   big bubbles, make your circle big.

Here's More: Pour some of your bubble
solution into a small
container and take your
bubbles with you! Just make
sure that your bubble wand
can fit into the opening! You
can also decorate your bubble
bottle with colorful ribbon,
or glue on cute felt shapes.

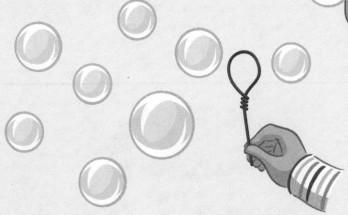

To make more bubble
wands, you can use
objects around your house.
Try a plastic funnel or
unfolded paper clips formed
into different shapes and sizes.

4. Dip your bubble wand into the bubble
   solution, and blow some of the berry
   best bubbles in Strawberryland!

Turn the page to make a project
that's spicy and sweet!

Apple Dumplin's Ornaments

You can hang these applesauce cinnamon cutouts in your room, or give them as gifts to your family and friends.

What You Need

- 3 tablespoons ground cinnamon
- 3 tablespoons applesauce
- Small bowl
- Plastic spatula or spoon
- Non-stick cookie sheet
- Cookie cutters
- Straw
- Optional: Washable paint, puffy paint, 12-inches of ribbon or string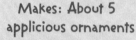

Makes: About 5 applicious ornaments

(Although these ornaments smell berry yummy, remember they're not for eating!)

1. To make the dough, pour the ground cinnamon and the applesauce into a small bowl, and mix. Let the dough sit for about 5 minutes to firm.

2. Place the dough onto a cookie sheet, and flatten it out so it's about as thick as a pencil.

3. Cut out some fun shapes in the dough using cookie cutters.

4. Remove the extra dough from around the cookie cutters, roll it into a ball, and flatten it to make more cutouts.

5. To hang the ornaments, use the straw to make a small hole toward the top of the cutouts, before the dough dries.

6. Place the cutouts on the cookie sheet in a warm place. It could take a few days for the dough to dry and harden completely. Turn the cutouts over occasionally to make sure that they dry flat.

Here's More: You can use the paints from your Apple Craft Kit, along with puffy paints, to decorate the shapes! Once dry, tie colorful ribbons on your ornaments so you can hang them.

Turn the page for two of
Apple Dumplin's juiciest treats!

Apple Dumplin's Juice Pops

Use your pops tray to make Apple Dumplin's favorite frozen treat!

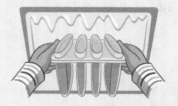

2. Place the tray in the freezer, and freeze the apple juice partially, for about 20 minutes.

What You Need

- 100% apple juice
- Pops tray
- 4 craft sticks

Servings: 4 sweet pops

3. Insert one craft stick into each mold, and freeze the juice until it's solid, about 3 hours.

1. Fill each of the pop molds with apple juice.

4. Remove each frozen juice pop from its mold by running warm water over it for a few seconds. Enjoy!

Apple Dumplin's Sweet Apple Sparkle

Apple Dumplin likes to help make this delicious apple drink!

1. Mix together the apple juice concentrate and the cold club soda in a pitcher using a large spoon.

2. Pour the apple sparkle into pretty juice glasses and serve!

What You Need

- 12-ounce can of 100% apple juice concentrate, partially thawed
- 1 liter of berry cold club soda
- Utensils: Large spoon, pitcher, juice glasses

Servings: 6 cups of sparkling juice

Did you know that eating a fresh apple can help quench your thirst? It's berry true!

This next recipe is crisp and sweet—just like a fresh apple!

Sweet 'n Crunchy Apple Crisp

This berry tasty treat combines the sweetness of applesauce and the crunchiness of granola!

What You Need

- ½ cup granola or crushed cereal
- ¼ cup applesauce
- 1 teaspoon brown sugar
- A sprinkle of ground cinnamon
- Utensils: Small cup or bowl, measuring cups and spoons

Makes: 1 crunchy serving

1. Pour the ¹/₂ cup of granola into a small cup or bowl.

2. Add the ¹/₄ cup of applesauce on top of the granola layer. Don't mix it!

3. Top the applesauce with a teaspoon of brown sugar.

4. Sprinkle ground cinnamon on top.

Here's More: You can add some vanilla ice cream to your apple crisp for an extra tasty treat!

5. Eat your berry sweet 'n crunchy apple crisp with a spoon!

Did you know that apples come in all different shades of red, green, and yellow?

Turn the page for a peanut butter sandwich that doesn't use bread!

Apple Dumplin's Apple Sandwiches

These tasty apple snacks are as fun to eat as they are to make!

What You Need

- 1 apple of your choice
- Paper towel
- Apple corer
- Cutting knife
- Butter knife
- Peanut butter or any other nut butter, like almond, cashew, or hazelnut
- 8 to 10 mini marshmallows per sandwich

Servings: 1 apple makes 2 berry sweet sandwiches

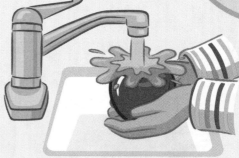

1. Wash your apple in cold water and dry it with a paper towel.

2. Ask an adult to core the apple using an apple corer, and then to cut the apple crosswise, about five times, into 1/2-inch slices. You won't need the end pieces of the apple. So go ahead and eat them!

3. Spread peanut butter onto two slices of apple. Will you use crunchy or smooth peanut butter? You decide!

6. Repeat steps 3 to 5, to make another delicious apple sandwich!

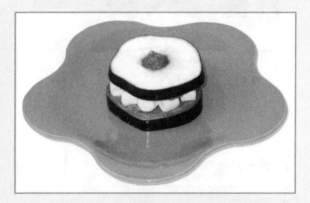

4. Sprinkle 8 to 10 mini marshmallows onto the peanut butter side of one of the apple slices.

Here's More: Instead of peanut butter and marshmallows, try your favorite cheese slices—like cheddar cheese—on an apple sandwich for an afternoon snack!

5. Sandwich the two slices together.

Turn the page for more berry fun food!

35

Berry Funny Apple Faces

Apple Dumplin' likes to snack on the toppings while she makes these adorable apple characters!

What You Need

- 1 well-shaped apple
- Paper towel
- Apple corer
- Creamy peanut butter or other nut butter
- 1 teaspoon raisins
- Toppings: Chocolate chips, roasted peanuts, small candies, circle-shaped cereal, mini marshmallows, strings of licorice, raisins, sunflower seeds
- Utensils: Small bowl, measuring spoons, spoon, butter knife

1. Wash your apple in cold water and dry it with a paper towel.

2. Ask an adult to core the apple.

3. In a small bowl, add 1 tablespoon of peanut butter and the raisins. Mix them together.

6. Decorate the face with any toppings you choose. Will you add a candy smile? A mini marshmallow nose? Round cereal eyes?

4. Fill the center of the apple with the peanut butter mixture. This will help to keep the apple face in place.

7. Now that you've played with your food, you can eat it!

5. Using a butter knife, scoop out some more peanut butter and spread it over the top of your apple to form a circle. This will be your apple face.

Here's a funny fact:
Did you know that apples are a natural toothbrush? It's berry true! Biting into a juicy apple can help make your smile sparkle!

Apple Dumplin's Answer Page

Apple Dumplin's Apple Cake Adventure (pages 24 and 25)

1. Airplane
2. Alarm Clock
3. Alligator
4. Alphabet Blocks
5. Angel Cake

6. Ants
7. Ape
8. Apple Dumplin'
9. Apples
10. Apple Tree

11. Aprons
12. Armchair
13. Animals
14. Apple Cake

More Sweet Strawberryland Adventures COMING SOON!

To Our Berry Sweet A-dorable Friend,

Did you have a berry good time on this all-apple adventure? Apple Dumplin', Apple Ducklin', and I really enjoyed your company! The crafts you made are so berry appealing, and the recipes were absolutely applicious! We hope you'll join us again on the next Strawberryland adventure coming soon!

Your berry best friends,

Strawberry Shortcake,

APPLE DUMPLIN',

and Apple Ducklin'